Anonymous

Short State of the Present Situation of the India Company

Anonymous

Short State of the Present Situation of the India Company

ISBN/EAN: 9783744689236

Printed in Europe, USA, Canada, Australia, Japan

Cover: Foto ©ninafisch / pixelio.de

More available books at **www.hansebooks.com**

SHORT STATE

OF THE

PRESENT SITUATION

OF THE

INDIA COMPANY,

BOTH IN

INDIA AND IN EUROPE;

WITH

An Examination into the probable Prospects of extricating
it from its present Difficulties.

———————

LONDON;

Printed for J. DEBRETT, opposite Burlington-House,
in Piccadilly. 1784.

SHORT STATE

OF THE

PRESENT SITUATION

OF THE

INDIA COMPANY.

THE affairs of the Eaſt-India Company, which have ſo long engroſſed the attention of the Public, but the real ſtate of which has been known to ſo few, are at length laid open ; and every individual who gives himſelf a little trouble, may, in a few days, be as completely maſter of the ſtate of their finances, as if he had been for years in the Direction.

The novelty of the ſubject, the difficulty of obtaining ſatisfactory information, and the various and contradictory accounts of the ſituation of the Company, both at home

B   and

and abroad, which common industry could not reconcile, have hitherto left India, in a manner, an unknown country to the bulk of Englishmen.

But the ill-judged boldness of the Court of Directors, in giving the public a state of the finances of the Company, and the active industry of the Committee of the House of Commons, in detecting their errors, and in comparing their accounts with the facts upon which they were said to be founded, has completely laid open, in the most authentic manner, the real state and condition of this Company. The golden dream is vanished, and the question is not now, what advantage is England to derive from India, but what is England to give to support India ? Or, what means are we to contrive, in order to prevent the tottering system of Indian Credit from falling to pieces, and perhaps involving the Public Credit of this Country in its ruins ?

From a comparison of the different reports laid before the Public, we are to learn
the

the real ftate of the credit and finances of
the Company, and to determine upon the
degree of affiftance requifite for its fupport;
and after all our inveftigations, it may, in
the minds of many, remain a doubt whether
any fupport will fave it from ruin..

The Committee of the Houfe of Commons, has confined itfelf to the making
obfervations on the affairs of the Company,
and has rather furnifhed materials for
making up a ftate of its finances, than given
any fuch ftate themfelves. But it will be
eafy to follow them through their obfervations, and to apply them fpecifically to the
different accounts made up by the Company.

In order to evince the fituation of the
Company, the Directors have laid before the
Public three different accounts, which, if
well founded, fhew their difficulties to be
temporary, and point out the means of
conquering them.

The firft of thefe is an eftimate of their

B 2   receipts

receipts and payments from January, 1784, to March, 1790 ; and by apportioning the great load of bills, now running upon them through different years, they ftate the means of paying them, provided they are allowed to poftpone fome of thefe bills for different periods, paying intereft to the bill-holders.

This Account, which is nothing more than a Cafh Account, would prove (if well founded) that the Company can go on till the year 1790, pay the bills which they knew of at the date of the report, and fuch future bills as are fuppofed to be neceffary for the carrying on their trade, a balance of cafh would remain in their hands, in March, 1790, of between two and three hundred thoufand pounds. But if, by any alteration of circumftances, the payments neceffary to be made by the Company fhould increafe, or the expected receipts diminifh, it is evident that the Company cannot go on, let the ftock of goods in their Warehoufes be great or fmall, without fome further affiftance than what is propofed. How far this is
likely

likely to be the cafe, a very fhort view of the obfervations of the Committee will point out.

The fecond Account contains a plan of trade and commerce to be carried on through the fucceeding years their Charter has to run, which is fo modified as to fhew that their future commerce, with the ftock of goods now on hand, will furnifh them with the means of procuring cafh, in order to make good their payments at the different periods when they become due. If this account is fallacious, and if their trade and commerce cannot be carried on, nor their ftock of goods on hand be difpofed of in the mode here pointed out, the whole fyftem muft fall to the round. For if their trade does not furnifh them with the means of finding cafh to make good their neceffary payments, the Company muft ftop.

The third Account produced, is an efti-mate of the probable furplus of revenue in India, after deducting all the charges of a peace eftablifhment, which furplus may in future

future be applied, firſt to the diſcharge of their debts in India, and afterwards, either to the providing of inveſtment, or to any other national purpoſe.

It is upon the accuracy and fidelity of all theſe different accounts, that the Public is to judge of the real ſituation of the Company, and how far the relief propoſed will anſwer the purpoſes intended by it. To give partial and temporary relief, is only encreaſing the evil, and doubling the calamity when it comes, at the ſame time that it leads the Public to overlook the real dangers that hang over it, and to take no means whatſoever to avert their calamitous effects.

It is, therefore, with the view that the Public may truly know the ſituation of the Company, and be able to decide juſtly between the Committee and the Directors, that I am led to ſtate the real ſituation of the Finances of the Company; and, ſurely, it is an object highly national, that every

man

man may be enabled to determine upon a
queftion of fo great magnitude and importance, both to the Public and to the
individual.

From a variety of caufes, bills to an immenfe amount, far exceeding the fums
allowed to be drawn for from India, by
Act of Parliament, have been accumulated
upon the Company, while quantities of
goods, the produce of the money borrowed
on thefe bills, are either arrived or are *expected* in England. The oftenfible plea of the
fervants abroad for this conduct is, that the
war had brought fo great a number of fhips
to India, that the allowing them to return
empty to Europe, or the detaining them
till the cargoes were provided in the regular
courfe of inveftment, would bring a ruinous
charge of freight and demurrage on the
Company; to obviate which, they were
induced to borrow money on bills upon
England, and with the money thus borrowed to provide cargoes for the fhips then
in India.

It

It is not material at prefent to examine into the wifdom of a tranfaction, which has for its bafis, the carrying on a * lofing trade with borrowed money, fubject to an intereft of eight *per cent.* from the time the money was advanced or fubfcribed, till the bills were drawn, and fubject to an intereft of five *per cent.* for the time they are propofed to be poftponed. It is fufficient to remark, that the uniform hardfhip complained of by the fervants of the Company, has been the difficulty of procuring the remittance of private fortunes to Europe, and that this plan, invented by themfelves, afforded an ample and an eafy mode of remittance to them, while it has been the caufe of that immenfe accumulation of bills, which now forms one of the embarrafsments

* Lofs on the Bengal inveftment, Appendix to the Ninth Report of the Select Committee,

1776	——	24,471
1777	— —	148,021
1778	— —	249,932
1779	— —	96,805

From this fhort ftate, the ruinous confequences of carrying on the Bengal trade with borrowed money is fufficiently apparent.

ments of the Company. It may be true, that goods either now are arrived, or are soon expected to arrive in England, purchased with the money thus borrowed, but if the trade is by no means a gaining one, and if the market for Indian goods is limited, the diftrefs of the Company muft be great, as the bills muft be paid before the goods from the produce of which they ought to be paid, can be difpofed of. To ✓ remedy this evil, the Directors propofe firft to poftpone paying to the Public the fum of 924,862l. now due for duties. Secondly, To poftpone the bills to fuch periods as their receipts will enable them to difcharge them. Thirdly, To detain from the Public the fum of 100,000l. ftill remaining due, for the laft renewal of the Charter. And, Fourthly, So to conduct their future exports and imports, as to enable them to difpofe of the accumulated load of goods foon expected in England. ∧

But if this complicated fcheme of commerce and finance is erroneous in any material article, the fabric muft tumble to the

C   ground,

ground, and the embarrassments of the Company be encreased instead of being diminished. How far this is likely to be the case, the following observations will point out:

The cash estimate, or the estimate of receipts and payments offered by the Company in their first Report, proceeds upon the idea of postponing a sum amounting, with interest, to £.1,395,153 in bills, to a period of three years after they would regularly fall due, and by suiting their future payments to their receipts, to discharge a certain portion of them annually. They calculate that all these bills will be discharged before March, 1790, and every other demand upon them satisfied, and that balance of cash of £.201,000 will remain in their treasury, and a quantity of goods, equal in value to £.2,800,000 will remain in their warehouses at the time their charter expires.

This is, no doubt, a very flattering view of the condition of the Company, but an inspection of the report of the Committee, with

with the papers in the Appendix, will
fatisfy any mind lefs fanguine than that of
an India Director, of the fallacy of this
eftimate, without having recourfe to any of
thofe various contingencies which derange
the beft modelled fcheme, and which neceffarily muft arife in a fyftem fo great and
fo complicated as that of the Eaft-India
Company.

Accidents of whatever nature, and de-
viations from their plan, from whatever
caufe, are here laid afide, as totally foreign
to the calculation; (how far thefe are likely
to happen, may hereafter appear.) At prefent, I fhall only take notice of the arith-
metical errors of the plan, and ftate againft
this fuppofed balance, fuch fums as have
either been wholly omitted in the payments,
or have been over-ftated in the fuppofed
receipts.

The firft Report of the Directors had
fcarcely appeared, when they difcovered
that they had committed an error, by
omitting to ftate the fum of £.33,713 which

became

became due to the Public for cuftoms, and
for which they had not provided in their
eftimate; about the fame time, they difcovered that certain damaged goods had been
fold for the fum of £.26,561 lefs than they
had been eftimated at, and which, therefore,
were to be deducted from their receipts.—
Thefe two fums are very properly taken
notice of by the Directors, in the Second
Report, and they furnifh a ftrong inftance
of the fallibility of this fpecies of eftimate,
where no allowance is made for contingencies and unforefeen events.

While the Public are obliged to borrow
money at a heavy intereft, and to load the
individuals of this country with heavy taxes;
it appears extremely reafonable, that the
money they lend to the Eaft-India Company fhould be charged with an intereft, in
order to indemnify the Public from that
which they are obliged to pay. The Company is indebted to the Public in the fum
of £.924,862, which being poftponed for
the term required by the fituation of the
Company, would accumulate a fum of
£.172,240

£.172,240 for interest, and which either must be made a present of by the Public to the Company, or must form a charge on the cash estimate.

There is another sum of £.100,000, which, with six years interest, would form the sum of £.130,000, and is now due to the Public by the Company, for the renewal of their charter, and which either must form a charge against them, or must be given up by the Public.

The East-India Company have hitherto not been in the practice of insuring their ships and cargoes; but since they do not pay insurance, they must bear the loss when it arises, and that loss, whenever it happens, as it diminishes the quantity of their goods, also diminishes the stock from which the most considerable part of their receipts must arise. There is no way by which this chance of loss can be so fairly calculated, as by taking the price which is had for the insurance to India, by the Individuals who do insure. It is true, by not insuring, or,

in

in other words, by being their own infurer, the Company fave that part of the premium which forms the profit of the infurer; but whoever will calculate the chance of continued peace for fix years, and all the variety of accidents which may happen, will find that the common market price of infurance is the beft medium he can take, in computing the lofs and rifk of the Company. As this fum would be paid by the Company, if they infured, and is the beft meafure of their lofs, if they do not infure, it muft operate as an alteration of their account of receipts and payments, and form another deduction from the balance above-mentioned, of the fum of £.385,000.

But the material articles of the receipts of the Company, are the extent of its fales; and of its payments, the price of its exports. The accuracy of thefe form an effential feature in the eftimate propofed; in them, therefore, it is neceffary to be more exact. The Directors ftate their fales to amount, from an average of ten years, to the fum of £.3,300,000 per annum. It is remarkable, that

that no period of the history of the Company
would afford this average, but the one the
Directors have chofen; and it is well known, ✓
that the immenfe inveftments fent to Europe
in the years 1769, 1770, 1771, and 1772,
were fold by the Company at an immenfe
lofs; the fpeculations of fome of thofe in
the management of the Company at home,
required immenfe fales, in order to furnifh a
ground for high dividends. Thefe fpeculations ended in almoft the bankruptcy of
the Company, and with fuch fpeculations
the large fales were at an end. Fairnefs,
therefore, would lead us to ftrike thefe years
out of the period, and we fhall find the
average amount of the fales of the Company,
for the fix years, ending in 1778, not to
exceed £.3,190,000. But if we take a period, including two years before that taken
by the Directors, and two years after it, we
fhall find that the average was confiderably
lower, fcarcely amounting to £.3,150,000.
But if we take the period from 1765 to 1780,
and ftrike out the years of the large fales,
which flowed only from a principle fo deftructive, that no man could wifh to fee it
renewed,

renewed, we shall find the average amount
of the Company's sales does not exceed the
sum of £.3,027,000. In which ever point
of view, therefore, it is taken, the average
of the Directors is fallacious; and in so far
as it exceeds, the real average must form a
deduction from the receipts of the Company.
The fairest average amidst these seems to be
£.3,150,000, which, if just, will in six
years form a deduction from the receipts of
the Company of £.900,000.

It may be true, as has been asserted by
the Directors, that the quality of their goods
is improved; but if we consider that the
eyes of every nation in Europe are turned to
the trade of Bengal; that the competition
in the market of India is increased greatly;
and that the investments of the foreign Companies are furnished by those very servants,
whose duty it is to provide investment for our
own Company, for the sole purpose of remit-
ting home their own private fortunes, we shall
not see much reason to believe, that the
goods sold by the foreign Companies will
be inferior in quality to those imported into
England,

England; and we have abſolute certainty
that their cargoes are better aſſorted, ſince,
not many months ago, the Directors made
a formal charge againſt the Board of Trade
in Bengal, complaining of the ſingular circumſtance that the ſhips of foreign Companies were laden with every article which
ſold at a profit in Europe, while thoſe of
our own Company were filled with ſuch
goods only as ſold at a loſs *.

The payments to be made by the Company on account of goods exported, amount
to the ſum of £.370,000 *per ann.* according
to the Directors eſtimate, and to £.587,000

D

according

---

* There is alſo another circumſtance, which, no doubt, muſt
tend conſiderably to check and leſſen the ſales of the India
Company. It is but of late years that the manufacture of fine
cotton goods has been introduced into this country; from
the various improvements and machines invented for the
ſpinning of cotton, cotton-thread can now be had in this
country of a fineneſs ſuited to any manufacture. The
ingenuity of our weavers has not failed to make uſe of this
circumſtance, and at preſent cotton-muſlins are manufactured
in Britain at a price, and of a quality to rival thoſe brought
from Bengal. The manufacture is in an improving and
flouriſhing trade; and the more it flouriſhes, the more it
muſt leſſen the ſales of the Company.

according to the average of their exports for the twenty years laſt paſt. It affords but a melancholy proſpect to thoſe who value the export trade of this country, to conſider that the India Company cannot be reſcued from their preſent embarraſſment, unleſs the exports of England, are diminiſhed in the annual ſum to above two hundred thouſand pounds; but it may be juſtly doubted, whether, as the moſt conſiderable part of the exports of the Company conſiſt in military ſtores, cloathing for the troops, and other neceſſaries for the uſe of the ſettlements abroad, it is poſſible to make any ſuch reduction in the exports as is ſuppoſed by the Directors. The Chairman of the Company, indeed, ſtated in the Houſe of Commons, that the difference between the two eſtimates aroſe from bullion being included in the one, and not in the other; and that it is now not intended to export any more of that article in future.

If this were true, it would not be very eaſy to conceive how a trade in which great exportations of bullion were neceſſary,

could

could be carried on without such annual
fupply, and it would be ftill more difficult
to imagine, how Bengal could poffibly
fubfift for many years longer, while its
fpecie is continually exported, and none imported from any quarter of the globe. But
the fact is not true, for the Select Committee, in their Appendix to the Ninth
Report, have furnifhed us with an account
of the bullion exported for many years paft,
by the Eaft-India Company, which by no
means agrees with the ftatement given by
Mr. Smith, from 1758 to 1770 inclufive.
The average export of bullion to all the
Settlements of India, amounted to the fum
of £.146,894, and from 1771 to 1780
inclufive, it amounted to no more than the
fum of £.42,650. The ceafing to export
bullion will, therefore, in a very fmall degree
diminifh the exports of the Company, and
as that is the only mode ftated by the
Chairman in which they can be reduced, it
is fair to conclude, that the exports muft
remain in future what they have been for
many years paft. The exports for many
years paft amount at an average to £.587,000

per

per ann. therefore, the payments to be made on this account, will exceed that flated by the Directors in the annual fum of £.217,000 amounting in fix years to the immenfe fum of £.1,302,000.

The Directors in their eftimate take credit for the receipt of an annual fum of £.40,000. as the amount of the profit gained by the Company on the goods imported in private trade, and this fum is not eftimated at an average of paft years, but on a prospect of future ones, the indulgences to be given to the Captains are to be encreated: but it may be very doubtful, how far this encreafe of private trade, will not form a competition againft the Company itfelf at its own fales, while fo far from checking fmuggling, it will encourage it, and the large quantity allowed to be imported by the fervants of the Company, will only form a cover for a larger quantity to be fmuggled. As this regulation, therefore, is doubtful in its event, the moft accurate way of confidering the profits upon private trade is by an average of the paft, by which we fhall

find

find that it amounts to no more than
£.25,000, leaving a deduction from the receipts of the Company, of the sum of
£.15,000 *per ann.* amounting in six years
to the sum of £.90,000.

' Such then are the decreafes in receipts
and the encreafes of payments to which the
Company has to look, and which, if put
together, form a wonderful alteration in the
balance of cafh, which would remain to the
Company in March 1790.

The Directors firft Report ftates the balance to be £.201,302	Payments omitted in the Directors ftate.	
	Cuftoms not ftated in the firft Report	£.33,713
	Infurance	385,000
	To Government for intereft on duties	172,240
	To Government now due with intereft	130,000
	To the providing goods for export	1,300,000
	Receipts over ftated.	
	Sales in 6 years	900,000
	Private ditto	90,000
	Damaged goods	26,561
		£.3,037,514

If

If the diminution of the cash receipts of the Company, and the encrease of their cash payments, forms, a sum of above three million beyond what is stated in the Directors first Report, how is it possible to conceive, that the Company can go on, and answer the necessary demands that are upon them, by means of a proposed relief, which has for its ultimate object the retaining for some years a sum of public money without interest ? The idea of postponing the payment of Bills to periods after they fall due, will only afford the means of relief to the Company, in so far as it enables them to suit their payments to their receipts, and must be entirely inefficacious, since, with the postponements proposed, the receipts and payments cannot be brought in any degree to coincide.

But even admitting that this cash estimate were accurate, yet unless the proposition be true, which is assumed in it, " That " no more Bills than those provided for will " be drawn," the whole must fall to the ground. The estimate proceeds entirely
upon

upon this fuppofition, which is fo far from
being founded in fact, that Bills beyond √
what were known of by the Company, at
the time they framed their firft Report, to
the amount of £.1,275,184, have either
been actually drawn, or notice of their being to be drawn, has been received by the
Company.—It may be true, that goods equal ∧
in value to the amount of thefe Bills *may*
be provided in India, and even *may* arrive
in the warehoufes in England, (how far
this is likely to be the cafe will be afterwards confidered) but as the fales of the
Company cannot be encreafed, fo as to furnifh cafh for the difcharge of thofe Bills
when they become due, the Company muft
ftop for want of cafh to make their neceffary payments, and be under the neceffity
of applying again to Parliament, for a further pecuniary relief.

With regard to near one half of this fum,
accounts of which were received before the
Directors made their fecond Report, it is to
be obferved, that they there ftate, that it
will not make any alteration upon their cafh
eftimate, as by an alteration which has
taken

taken place in the duties and drawbacks upon muslins, the Company will save the sum of £.118,000 *per annum*; and the public by the new modification of the duties, will receive equal to the amount it now does. If this proposition is true, no doubt the Company will so far be gainers, but it may be remarked, that the experiment has been tried for a few months only, and upon so short a trial, the calculation is made for six years to come.

But with regard to the other half of this sum, the notice of which has been received since the publication of the second Report, either the bills must be paid, in which case an alteration equal to their amount must be made in the cash estimate of the Company; so they must be postponed to a period beyond the year 1790; a period so distant, that no bill-holder in his senses would agree to it. Or they must be sent back to Bengal, and thus form an addition to the bond debt there.—Or, they may be considered as a part of the bills, which were allotted to be drawn from India,

dia, for the future carrying on of the trade and commerce between that country and this. If they were taken to be a part of this fum, it may be true, that they will form no alteration in the cafh eftimate of the Company, but the confequences will be ftill more ruinous.

The propofed future plan for the trade of the Company, is to be reduced to a very low fcale indeed, if thefe bills are to be taken as part of thofe allotted for future commerce. The future inveftment from Bengal will be reduced almoft to nothing, and the manufacturer in that country muft be inevitably ruined.

He has been long accuftomed to a demand for his goods, equal to the inveftment provided by the Company. But if fuch quantities of goods are now accumulated from the fums collected for the bills drawn, or to be drawn, as to make it neceffary to ftop, in a great meafure, or perhaps totally, any Bengal inveftment for fome years, either the manufacturer muft perifh, and the trade be

E   ruined,

ruined, or the demand from the Englifh
Company ceafing, he muft get rid of his
goods at the beft price he can get from Foreigners, and as the market will be over-
ftocked with goods, from withdrawing the
Britifh demand, the Foreigners will pur-
chafe cheap, and of courfe be able to under-
fell the Company, in every market in Europe.

Thus, in which ever view this eftimate is
taken, it muft prove fallacious, unlefs a
greater relief in point of cafh is given to the
Company than the one now propofed. It
will only operate as a fhort and temporary
affiftance, totally inadequate to the objeét
intended.

It does not, however, neceffarily follow,
that the Company is in a ftate of ruin, becaufe it is not able to make good all the demands that are upon it, or, in other words,
becaufe it is not able to make its payments
and its receipts coincide.

It

It may happen that their Warehouses may be full of goods which cannot be disposed of, and their Treasuries abroad filled with money, that cannot be remitted to Europe ; nothing, indeed, can be a stronger proof of the false system upon which the great investment loans have been made, and upon which the trade of the Company has of late been carried on, than the total impossibility of accommodating their payments to their receipts, but it is not necessarily a proof of real poverty and ruin. The real situation of the Company, is to be gathered from a review of their proposed scheme of trade, an examination into the funds provided for investment, and a discussion of the state of their possessions abroad.

In considering any plan of future commerce, to be carried on by the East-India Company, there is one object beyond the mere practicability of the scheme to be attended to, and that is the relative operation which any proposed plan will have upon the situation of Bengal, and the effects it

may

may have on the future refources of that country.

It is extremely practicable that a Company which feels the immediate preffure of the demand at home, may invent a plan of trade and a fyftem of commerce, which may not only be plaufible, but even advantageous for a few years, but which in the end muft prove ruinous to the country from which it is drawn, and produce the deftruction of that very Company, the profperity of which it was invented to promote.

The circumftances of the joint character of Sovereign and Merchant, which are fo incompatibly united in the Eaft-India Company, and the certainty which experience gives us, that the real intereft of Bengal, and of courfe the true intereft of the Company, has been often facrificed to prefent views and immediate objects, will lead us to watch with attention any new fcheme that is propofed for the trade and commerce of India. And I am afraid, we fhall find, upon inveftigation, that the plan propofed

pofed by the Directors, is not only fallacious in the eftimate it gives of the prefent
funds of the Company, but doubtful in the
practicability of its execution, and perhaps
ruinous and oppreffive in its effects.

' The firft object, however, is to confider
the amount of the funds, before we confider
the nature of them.

The eftimate ftates a fum of £.5,811,049
as the total amount of the fund provided for
the feafon 1783-4. But as that fum has,
from fubfequent events, partly mentioned
in the fecond Report of the Directors, and
partly taken notice of in the Report of the
Committee, undergone a variety of alterations, it may be proper to ftate thefe at
length, in order to give a true knowledge
of the real amount of the funds propofed for
inveftment.

Firft then, there is to be deducted from
this fund, the following fums, mentioned in
the fecond Report of the Directors.

The

The amount of the produce of the falt
and opium, which inftead of being applied
to the purpofe of inveftment, was applied
to the current fervice of the year, £.450,000
Certificates from Bengal,   115,560
Bills from Bombay, which were ⎫
  divided among the Bond- ⎬ 45,000
  holders, - - - - - ⎭
Bills not drawn from China, - 150,000
              ————————
              £. 760,560

  But there is to be added to the fund the
fum of fifteen and thirty-five lacks, fubfcribed
in April and Auguft, 1783, and mentioned
in the fecond Report of the
Directors, - - - £. 562,500
Cargoes from Bombay, - - 100,000
       from Madras, - - - 37,000
50 Lacks fubfcribed in Nov. 1783, 562,500
              ————————
             1,262,000
              760,560
              ————————
              £. 501,440
Thefe alterations, therefore, will give us
the fum of above five hundred thoufand
                   pounds,

pounds, to be added to the fund provided
for the fupplying of inveftment, which will
ftand thus :

Sums ftated in the firft report   5,811,049
Add the balance above ftated   501,440

Total fund for the inveft- ⎫
ment, 1783-4   ⎬   6,312,489

It is not a little remarkable, that this
propofed fund fhould, for one of its firft
articles, comprehend a fum of £.213,000,
which does not belong to the Company.—
It is called the produce of the Dutch inveftment, which fum, fo far from actually
belonging to them, is the fubject of litiga-
tion between them and the captors; the
greatnefs of the amount forms the principal
reafon why the Company contend it be-
longs to them, while the troops who took
Chinfura, and the Captain of one of his
Majefty's frigates who affifted them, fup-
ported in his claim by Sir Edward Hughes,
infift that the amount of the booty can
never make any alteration on the right of
the captors. To ftate that which is claimed
by

by others, as the exclusive property of
the Company, in the very outset of the
estimate, does not imprefs us with the most
favourable idea of its subfequent accuracy,
or fidelity. In order to know whether the
funds faid to be provided for inveftment
were actually applied to that purpofe, the
Committee of the Houfe of Commons have
laid before the Public an eftimate * of all
the cargoes that are expected to be fhipped
for. England from India for the feafon,
1783-4, which amount to no more than
£.4,240,178.

From this it is apparent, that the funds
applicable to the purpofes of inveftment,
exceed the inveftment actually provided
in no lefs a fum than £.2,073,311. For
this deficiency, it is not eafy to account in
any manner at all fatisfactory. The fact is
not ftated in any report of the Directors,
who only lay before the Public the amount
of the funds fuppofed to be provided, and
the

* Furnifhed to them by the accountants at the India-
Houfe.

the Committee confefs, that they are at a lofs how to explain fo material a variation.

It is poffible, that part of the fum may have been advanced to manufacturers, as is the cuftom in India, and from the latenefs of the advances, the goods could not be provided time enough to be fhipped in the year, 1783-4, but will remain to form part of the inveftment of a future year; it is impoffible, however, to fuppofe that a fum above two millions either has been, or can be accounted for in this way.

The advances made to the manufacturer in the times of the greateft inveftments, could not account for a fourth of this fum.

We know, that by much the greateft part of the fubfcriptions to thefe inveftment loans were not made in money *, but were adjufted by adjufting of debts due to the fub-

F   fcribers

* Vide Board of Trade's Letter, 4th November, 1783.

fcribers by the Government in Bengal, and by the paying in of orders on the Treafury, which were in their hands; the mode, therefore, that has been adopted, was to give bills on England to the fubfcribers, equal to the debts and orders thus adjufted, and to grant to the Board of Trade a credit equal to the amount paid in, which they were to ufe, by giving orders on the Treafury for fuch fums as they might have occafion to pay for the goods they purchafed. A variety of obfervations naturally prefent themfelves to our minds, upon the firft view of this complicated mode of raifing money, and may lead us to a variety of conjectures, in order to account for the deficiency above ftated.

It is well known that the Treafury orders in Bengal, a fpecies of circulation fimilar to that of Exchequer bills in this country, were at a difcount of four or five per cent. and it may not only be poffible, but probable, that in fuch circumftances, the Board of Trade could not circulate the orders they

they wifhed to iffue, and of courfe could not provide the inveftment propofed *.

We further know, from the fecond Report of the Directors, that all the money procured by the inveftment loans of fifteen and thirty five lacks in April and Auguft, 1783, was, in the firft inftance, applied to the current fervice of the year, and in lieu of it a credit on the Treafury given to the Board of Trade; if this credit either was not, or could not be ufed, this will alfo account, in fome meafure, for the deficiency.

Which ever way we turn the fubject, we fhall find its difficulties inexplicable; but this intricacy will certainly lead us not to

give

---

* If thefe credits on the Treafury were nothing more than mere anticipations of current revenue of the year, there will be no encreafe to the debt abroad; but if they are, as there is every reafon to fuppofe, the means of bor owing money, and not to be paid out of the revenue as it comes in, then there will remain a debt due in Bengal eqnal o heir amount, which muft be added to the debt in Inoi , but which we fhall fee hereafter, when we come to confiuer the debts due by the Company abroad is no where carried to account.

give the Company credit for the whole amount of the fund provided for inveft-·ment, when we fee fo great, and fo irreconcileable a difference between that and the inveftment actually provided; and when, from the mode in which the fubfcriptions were paid in, there is reafon to believe, that the whole operation of the loan would end· in liquidating out-ftanding demands upon the Bengal Government, by bills upon England.

It is the more neceffary to be cautious upon this head, fince the goods which ought to be provided with this two millions are valued at double that fum, when they come to be fold in England, and of courfe· are taken as the fund for fupplying the Company at home, with a fum in cafh, amounting to above four millions.

In the eftimate of future commerce, the fum of £.450,000 *per annum*, is regularly taken as a commercial profit by the Company, and applied to the purpofe of inveft-ment,

ment, and arifes from what is called the
profit on falt and opium. The falt is entirely new as an article of revenue, to any
thing near the extent here propofed, which,
great as it is, is ftill inferior to the fum
faid to be raifed from it. The old revenue
realized from falt, did not exceed a fixth
part of what it now is faid to produce, fince
the whole falt has been manufactured and
fold for the Company's benefit.

The Company is the fole proprietor of
all the grounds where falt can be made,
their fervants manufacture it, and fell it at
the rifque of the Company. It is difficult
to conceive a more perfect monopoly of a
neceffary article, and it is undoubtedly in
the power of the fervants of the Company,
to raife from this revenue any fum they
think proper.

It may be true, that the price of falt is
not yet raifed to fuch a pitch, as to become
oppreffive to the natives, but it is difficult
to conceive how a revenue can be raifed
from feven lacks of rupees to near fifty,
without

without some considerable degree of injustice; and if this immense increase arises from concentrating in the Company the former profits of the farmers of the salt districts, without increasing the price to the consumer, it is equally difficult to conceive, how the farmers of districts immediately under the eye of the servants of the Company, could have, for so many years, been permitted quietly to enjoy so immense a profit. Before, therefore, we can give credit for this immense sum, as an article for the provision of future investment, it will certainly merit a more minute enquiry than it hitherto has undergone, or, indeed, than the materials in England render practicable, in order to ascertain whether this monopoly of a necessary of life, be not the engine of oppression, and whether that, which the History of Bengal teaches us has often been employed for the worst of purposes, is not already converted to the same ends.

With regard to the opium monopoly, the profit from that contract has never yet exceeded £.25,000, and yet, from the produce

[39]

duce of one year only, it is ſtated in future
at £.50,000; and it is a miſerable ſhift to
increaſe revenue, when the Government of
a great country becomes ſmugglers, as the
Government of Bengal does become, when
it propoſes to increaſe the trade in opium
by ſmuggling it into China *.

But if we ſuppoſe it poſſible, or expe-
dient, that ſuch monopolies be allowed to
exiſt, the mode the Company propoſe to
uſe the ſum thus gained, appears perfectly
chimerical. In future, the trade between
China and England, which for years paſt
has been carried on by the intervention of
near £.300,000 a-year in bills, is to be
carried

* The Directors, in their Firſt Report, as we have ſeen,
take into that eſtimate for the proviſion of inveſtment, the
whole produce of the ſalt and opium for the year 1783-4;
were any thing wanting to convince us of the total fallibility
of this ſpecies of eſtimate, which muſt, for its accuracy,
depend upon a thouſand events and contingencies, that the
wiſeſt man cannot foreſee, nor the moſt prudent prevent,
the obſervation contained in the Second Report, would
operate complete conviction. In the month of February,
the Directors ſtate to the Houſe of Commons, that they have
reaſon to think that the ſum of £.450,000 will be applicable
to a particular purpoſe; and in May they are forced to con-
feſs, that this whole ſum has been applied to other purpoſes.

carried on by the drawing for no greater a
fum than a little above £.100,000 *per ann.*
Such a reftriction in point of drawing bills
is abfolutely neceffary, in order to give the
eftimate of receipts and payments any colour
of probability. But as the trade cannot be
carried on without fome medium, the project is formed of tranfporting annually the
fum of £.250,000 from India to China,
which is ftated by the Directors, as if it
were as eafy to carry into effect, as it is to
propofe. That there is little commercial
intercourfe between Bengal and China, is a
fact perfectly notorious; and if any evidence
of it were required, it would be fufficient
to ftate, that, upon every occafion, the Directors have encouraged their Factors in
China to draw bills upon Bengal, and yet
they never have been able to draw above
£.10,000 *per annum.* How this is to be
increafed at once to £.250,000, muft remain
a problem, till the Directors chufe to folve
it.

The fmuggling of opium may indeed do
a little, till the Chinefe Government fhall
detect

detect and punish the servants of the Com-, pany; and some little commerce may be carried on, through the medium of the Eastern islands.

But it is impossible to imagine how this is to amount to £.250,000 *per annum*, unless money is to be collected in Bengal, and sent as bullion to China.

That the money of Bengal has been de-creasing for years past, is a melancholy truth ; and this country is not likely to re-medy the evil, by stopping all remittances from Europe, and nothing was wanting to put the finishing hand to its ruin, but the establishing a regular mode for the expor-tation of the specie which is taken from the wretched inhabitants, by a monopoly of a necessary of life.

Formerly specie flowed into Bengal from a variety of channels. Europe furnished a large quantity ; the commerce with Delhi, Agra, and Lahore, which were formerly in a flourishing state, and with the dominions

G   of

of Oude, which have uniformly decreafed in profperity in the proportion of their connection with the Europeans, gave a confiderable fupply, while the trade with the Weft of India and Perfia, was equally beneficial. At prefent not only are all thefe channels cut off, and the internal trade of India totally at a ftand, but the new project of the Directors is to eftablifh a regular channel for the exportation of fpecie from Bengal, which will foon complete the ruin of that diftreffed country.

The fcheme further proceeds upon an idea of confining the inveftment from Bengal, to a fum little exceeding £.300,000, inftead of near a million, which it formerly amounted to. It is true, that the fyftem of inveftment drawn from revenue, operates in the nature of a tribute paid by Bengal to Europe, and, it may be faid, that reducing the inveftment will operate as a reduction of tribute, and thus be beneficial to Bengal; whatever effect this may have, after a confiderable period, on the profperity of Bengal, at prefent it muft, as has been already

already hinted, end in the ruin either of the Company, or the Bengal manufacture. If this fudden decreafe of the inveftment falls entirely on the manufacturer, he muft inevitably ftarve. The ruin of the manufacturer neceffarily brings along with it decreafe of revenue, and thus operates to render all the hopes from the furplus of Indian revenue entirely vifionary. In the progrefs of this ruin, the manufacturer, in the ftruggles of neceffity, will be compelled to fell at an inferior price to foreigners, and to Englifhmen who fupply foreigners: and this muft operate againft the Company in their fales at home.

If foreigners carried on their trade through the medium either of bullion, or of commodities exported from Europe, fuch a trade, proceeding upon commercial principles, might, and certainly would be more advantageous to Bengal, than the fyftem of inveftment drawn from it by Britain; but the misfortune is, that the trade of foreigners to Bengal, is almoft equally deftructive of its profperity as that carried on by the Englifh

G 2   Company,

Company; little or nothing is carried out.
The capital is furnished by the servants of
the India Company, and the operation of
their trade only differs from the trade of the
Company in this: they draw from Bengal
that which is acquired by extortion, while
the Company draw that which is acquired
by revenue.

The lessening then of the investment
from Bengal, will only facilitate the remittance of private fortunes, by forcing the
manufacturer to part with his goods at any
price he can get, or to starve. By faci-
litating the transportation of private fortunes, it will accelerate the ruin of that
country, while the foreigner who brings
the goods to Europe, accelerates the ruin of
the Company at home, by underselling it in
every market.

Perhaps nothing will in the end operate
so much towards the ruin of Bengal, as the
immense investment loans that have lately
been made. While the war in other parts
of India formed a severe drain from Bengal:
the

the facility which thefe loans gave to every one to fend his fortune to Europe, has left Bengal, at a time when its credit was oppreffed and fhaken, without one fingle fhilling of the private fortune of almoft any European in India.

So much then for this Second Eftimate of the Directors, which, if carried into execution, appears doubtful in the amount of the fums provided, impracticable in fome of its points, and ruinous in all. We fhall now proceed to take a view of the probable neat furplus that will remain to the Company, from their revenue in India, after deducting their expences, and providing a fund for the payment of their debts and other demands, to which they are fubject abroad.

The bond debt at the different Prefidencies, amounts to the fum of £.4,799,703. The arrears due by the Company at Madras, amount, by Lord Macartney's accounts, to above £.500,000. The arrears of Pifcufh due to the Nizam, and promifed to be paid

paid, amount to £.330,000. The demand of the Public on the revenue in India, for the expence of victualling the King's ships, is £.566,903. The pay due to the Public, for troops lent to the Company, amounts to £.215,000; all these sums must be added to the bond debt in India, and will form a capital of £. 6,411,646, exclusive of many further demands for winding up the war, exclusive of that sum of Treasury orders and demands upon the Company, which, as has been already stated, there is every reason to apprehend, exist to a considerable amount unprovided for; and exclusive of a sum of thirty lacks, which, even according to the most favourable state lately transmitted by Mr. Hastings, the revenue of 1783-4, will fall short of the demands, or, of 120 lacks, according to the report of the Select Committee.

The Interest usually paid upon the Company's debt in India, is eight *per cent.* which upon a capital of £. 6,400,000, would amount to £.512,000 *per annum.*

The

The neat revenue fuppofed to remain to the Company in India, after deducting the charges of collection, the civil, military, and marine charges, amounts, according to the Directors eftimate, to the fum of £.1,091,546. It is from this furplus, if fairly ftated, that both the principal and intereft of this immenfe load of debt is to be paid, and it is therefore a point of importance to examine whether its amount is fairly ftated, and the charges upon the revenues abroad accurately made.

First then, a fum equal to the whole intereft of all the debt in India, muft be ftated as an annual charge upon the revenue in India, as from that only it can be paid.

Secondly, The Directors ftate the civil charges of Bengal to amount to a fum of £.350,000 in the year. However, thefe charges in the year 1777-8, amounted to above £.400,000, and in the year 1780-1 to the fum of £.589.000. It is true, that the Directors object to this laft year being

being taken as the amount of the civil charges, as in that year a confiderable payment to the fon of the Rajah of Barar, was included in the civil charges, which ought not to be confidered as an annual payment, but the Chairman of the India Company ftated in the Houfe of Commons, that they might in future amount to about £.427,000 *per annum*. Therefore, according to his account, the civil charges are under-ftated by the Directors in their account, the fum of £.77,000, which will form a further charge upon the Revenue in India.

The revenue at Madras, is ftated by the Directors to amount to £.600,000, *per annum*, but from the average of paft years, from 1771, to 1780, it amounts only to the fum of £.484,000.

It is not eafy to imagine, why the Directors chufe to ftate it at the above fum, but furely it is not very unreafonable to fuppofe, that a country which has been fo

long

long the feat of war and defolation, will not yield a higher revenue, than it did in time of peace and profperity, therefore, a fum of £.116,000 muft further be deducted, from the fuppofed neat furplus in India.

The civil charges at Madras, are ftated by the Directors to amount to £.60,000. Lord Macartney, however, ftates them at prefent at above £. 100,000. And in the eftimate he has fent home, of the fuppofed ftate of that fettlement at the end of three years peace, he ftates them at £.120,000, it is not therefore extravagant to ftate them at the annual fum of £.100,000, which will form a further deduction of £.40,000.

The fum which Bencoolen and Bombay have annually required, over and above their own revenues, appears from an average of many years paft, to be to the firft, £.59,000: to the latter, £.246,000. Thefe fupplies are, however, ftated by the Directors at £.50,000, and £.226,000; which leave an additional charge on the fuppofed furplus revenue in India of £.35,000. Deducting

H   all

all thefe feveral fums, from the furplus ftated by the Directors, it will ftand thus :

	Sums to be deducted.
Surplus ftated by the Directors, £.1,091,546	The intereft of £.6,400,000, at eight per cent. £.512,000
	Civil charges at Bengal, un-der-ftated, 77,000
	Madras revenue, over-ftated, 166,000
	——— Civil charges under-ftated, 40,000
	Supplies to Bombay and Bencoolen,
Total fums to be deducted, 780,000	underftated 35,000
Neat furplus, £. 311,546	£.780,000

It will, however, be obferved, that in confidering the deductions to be made from the India revenue, it is fuppofed that the military and marine charges, and the expence of fortifications, are actually reduced to that fum, which the Directors in their eftimate, ftate them to be reduced to, and it is even probable that œconomy and a pacific fyftem may render it fafe to reduce them lower than they

'they are ftated. And alfo that the revenue
in India actually produces at prefent, and
will produce in future, the fum at which it
is taken at by the Directors. But it will
alfo be obferved, that in order to form this
furplus of £.300,000, the payments made
to the Company from Oude and Benares,
and which lately have been encreafed, the
one from 34 to 54 lacks, and the other
from 22 to 44 lacks, are here included at
their higheft amount; and cre it, for the
full receipt of the whole fubfidy is taken;
how far this is confiftent with juftice, or
even with the poffibility of payment, is not
now to be difcuffed fully. When Raja Cheit
Sing whofe tribute was formerly 22 lacks,
was called upon by the Bengal Government,
for an additional pa, ment of 5 lacks *per
ann.* he complained of it, not only as an act
of injuftice, but as ruinous and oppreffive to
the country he governed ; now the tribute is
raifed to double its former amount, and the
country is fuppofed to pay the advanced
fum with eafe, when it was with difficulty
that the former fmaller fum was raifed from
it. The diftrict of Benares though rich, is

very

very limited in extent, and the drawing the immenfe fum of near £. 500,000 from fuch an extent of country, cannot but foon end in its ruin.

The fubfidy from Oude has alfo been confiderably encreafed; what probability there is of obtaining this advanced fum from a country which was always in arrears, when it paid a fmaller fubfidy, which is now reprefented by its Prince, to be in a ftate of mifery and famine, and which has, between the year 1774 and the year 1780, decreafed in its profperity and diminifhed in its revenue, to the amount of 65 lacks a year, as appears by the comparative ftate of its revenue, publifhed by the Committee, time muft difcover.

But it is not the part of a very gloomy politician to prognofticate, that a Company which trufts its profperity to fuch precarious and doubtful refources, has but a fmall chance of diminifhing the immenfe load of debt that now hangs over it.

This

This surplus is not only suppofed to be really efficient, but the affairs of the Company in the Eaft, are fuppofed to be already, and to continue in uninterrupted profperity, peace, and good Government for fix years to come, no allowance whatever is made for the variety of contingencies, which muft unavoidably occur in the beft regulated and the leaft complicated fyftem of Government; if they do happen, this furplus of £.300,000, fuch as it is, is the only fund to which the Company can look, to extricate itfelf from its prefent embarafsment, and to provide againft future diftrefs.

It is a melancholy truth, that according to Mr. Haftings's laft letter, peace is not yet eftablifhed in India The Madras Government was preparing to take the field, and fuch is the ftate of the Company, that no war, however profperous, can tend to its benefit Tippo Saib may be defeated, and perhaps his dominions divided amongft the confederates againft him, but the common expences of war will encreafe the embaraffments

raffments of the Company, while the only effect of deftroying the empire of Tippo Saib, will be to increafe the power, and to bring into our neighhourhood, by much the moft formidable of the Indian States. The fituation of India, with the natural jealoufies which have taken deep root in the breafts of the native Princes ; the fhort-fighted policy which leads them to grafp at prefent power, and prefent enjoyment, and the precarious and fluctating nature of defpotic authority, which too often induces its poffeffors to feek prefent advantage at the expence of future fecurity; with the deep private intereft, which many of the Europeans in India have in wars and confufion, does not afford us the fureft profpect of uninterrupted peace and undifturbed profperity.

Tippo Saib is actually at war; the Raja of Berar, whofe friendfhip we formerly purchafed at an immenfe price, is jealous of our power, and has undertaken a journey to Poona, while Mr. Chapman our Refident, at his Court, found his fituation fo unpleafant,

fant, from the jealoufy of the Raja, that he thought it prudent to folicit his recal. Scindia who has of late been fo much our friend in all the tranfactions relative to the Marhatta peace, has at the fame time afforded a fafe and fecure afylum to Cheit Sing, who was expelled his dominions by our authority, and is at this moment carrying on a war againft the miferable Rana of Gohud, flights our mediation, and threatens to exterminate him for no other reafon than his attachment to us during the Marhatta war: with fuch difpofitions in the three moft powerful native Princes, who border upon our dominions, the certainty of fix years peace, is at beft but a precarious hope, which neither the prefent fituation nor the paft experience of Indian hiftory will juftify.

Such then is the fituation of the Company, from all the accounts that are offered to the Public; an embaraffed fituation at home, an extenfive and exhaufted territory abroad, and a doubtful and precarious peace. Great, indeed, muft be the talents, and fevere the

œconomy

œconomy which can retrieve its affairs, and remedy all thofe evils which a feries of misfortune and mifmanagement has entailed upon it.

F I N I S.

www.ingramcontent.com/pod-product-compliance
Lightning Source LLC
Chambersburg PA
CBHW030719110426
42739CB00030B/997